breakfast

marie claire

breakfast

jody vassallo

marie claire

THUNDER BAY
P·R·E·S·S

San Diego, California

introduction

The renowned economist J. K. Galbraith once observed, "It takes some skill to spoil a breakfast," going on to cheekily add that "even the English can't do it." And it's true that in the mornings, we're often happy with the easiest of no-brainer foods—toast, cereal from a box, or scrambled eggs and bacon, perhaps. Even for those who don't, won't, or claim they *can't* cook, breakfast is the simplest of meals to get right; we can all buy jelly, slice fresh fruits, spoon out yogurt and granola, or combine smoothie ingredients in a blender. Sometimes, though, the occasion calls for a little more inspiration— it's easy to fall into a breakfast-time rut. Enter *Marie Claire Breakfast*. Here you'll find lots of ideas for creating all kinds of delicious morning meals; from those in the gratifyingly easy Quick Ideas section to the heartier sweet or savory breakfast options. Chic, easy, and flavorful, these recipes represent the best of modern cooking. Ingredients are chosen from an international pantry (arugula, halloumi, salmon roe, couscous, and panettone, for example); flavors are made fresh and zingy by the generous use of herbs, spices, and fabulous seasonal produce; and the presentation is clean, simple, and tantalizing. You'll love the idea of entirely stress-free dishes such as sheep's milk yogurt served with a swirl of strawberry puree, broiled portobello mushrooms with garlic and chili, or that most sexy of fruits, the pomegranate, drizzled with rose water and apple juice. When friends or family stay for the the night, you can easily turn breakfast the next morning into a fun social occasion by whipping up something even more special: corn fritters with crispy prosciutto, maybe, or hearty huevos rancheros. Poached stone fruits and a batch of passion fruit sugar muffins will hit the sweet spot—although if you feed them this well, your guests may never want to go home! For the traditionalist at heart, too, there's plenty here to satisfy, with livened-up versions of breakfast-time classics. You'll find new spins on all the old favorites—a BLT bursts with sunny, Mediterranean flavors (provolone, mortadella, and basil), good old pork sausages come with sweet potato and bell pepper rosti, and even oatmeal is elevated to new heights with the addition of cinnamon, caramel, and figs.

contents

8   quick ideas

14   savory

92   sweet

156   index

quick ideas

fresh mixed berries standing alone

chilly iced chocolate

toasted panettone served with sweet
sage, apple, and cinnamon toddies

halved finger bananas drenched with light
corn syrup and finished with chopped
macadamia nuts

espresso with a pinch of ground
cinnamon and cinnamon sticks

sheep's milk yogurt with pureed
strawberries stirred through

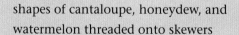

shapes of cantaloupe, honeydew, and
watermelon threaded onto skewers

fresh passion fruits frozen in their cups

quick ideas

steamed asparagus topped with crispy
pancetta and hard-boiled quail eggs

broiled apricots served with apricot and
bran breakfast shake (see page 93)

colorful fruit platter using mango, guava, grapes,
honeydew, kiwifruit, and ripe baby pears

wedges of red papaya drizzled with
tangy lime juice

slices of dried fruit sprinkled with brown sugar and broiled until caramelized

fresh figs and dates atop thick yogurt drizzled with honey and sprinkled with toasted pine nuts

pineapple and star fruit slices with maple syrup and shaved, toasted coconut

luscious red pomegranates drizzled with combined rose water and apple juice

quick ideas

fresh banana and ripe mango blended with
vanilla soy milk and honey-drizzled yogurt

chilled fresh guava juice

ginger ale and fresh pineapple juice punch
with ginger, strawberries, and mint leaves

decadent caffe latte infused with a
vanilla bean

cups of ginger tea with lemongrass
swizzle sticks

champagne with strawberries and blackberries

glasses of cardamom caffe latte
accompanied by a generous nip
of Frangelico

vodka, tomato juice, a few drops of Tabasco,
Worcestershire sauce, and celery salt

mediterranean blt

4 small vine-ripened tomatoes, halved
1 garlic bulb, halved
1 tablespoon extra-virgin olive oil, plus extra for drizzling
sea salt and cracked black pepper, to taste
1 small handful fresh basil leaves
1 loaf crusty bread
8 slices provolone cheese
8 slices mortadella
2 handfuls arugula
balsamic vinegar, for drizzling

Preheat the oven to 400°F. Put the tomatoes and garlic in a roasting pan and drizzle with 1 tablespoon of oil. Sprinkle with sea salt and cracked black pepper and roast for 40 minutes, or until the garlic is soft and the tomatoes are slightly dried. Add the basil leaves and continue cooking for 5 minutes, or until the leaves are crisp. Remove from the oven.

Cut four thick slices from the loaf of crusty bread and lightly toast on both sides. Peel the roasted garlic cloves and spread half onto the toast. Top with the provolone, mortadella, arugula, basil, and roasted tomatoes. Sprinkle with the remaining roasted garlic, drizzle with a little extra-virgin olive oil and balsamic vinegar, and serve immediately.

SERVES 4

salmon, dill, and camembert frittata

12 eggs
1/2 cup grated Parmesan cheese
1 1/2 cups whipping cream
6 scallions, sliced
8 oz smoked salmon
1/4 cup chopped fresh dill, plus a few sprigs for garnish
4 oz Camembert cheese, sliced
grated zest of 1 lemon

Preheat the oven to 350°F. Lightly grease and line a 9-inch springform pan. Lightly beat the eggs, Parmesan, and cream, and stir in the scallions. Thinly slice most of the smoked salmon and add it to the egg mixture, leaving a bit for garnish. Add the chopped dill. Pour the mixture into the pan and place the pan on a baking sheet. Bake for 50–60 minutes, or until the frittata has set.

Allow to cool slightly before removing from the pan. Arrange the remaining smoked salmon and all of the sliced Camembert decoratively in the center of the frittata. Sprinkle with lemon zest and serve with dill sprigs.

SERVES 6–8

fried green tomatoes with halloumi

18 oz halloumi cheese, cut into ½-inch-thick slices
2 garlic cloves, crushed
2 tablespoons lemon juice
1 tablespoon balsamic vinegar
3 tablespoons extra-virgin olive oil
8 oz cherry tomatoes
8 oz teardrop tomatoes, halved
4 green tomatoes, cut into thick slices
½ cup buttermilk
1 cup polenta
vegetable oil, for panfrying
2 handfuls arugula
2 teaspoons marjoram leaves, to serve

Put the halloumi, garlic, lemon juice, vinegar, and olive oil in a nonmetallic bowl and marinate for at least 3 hours. Drain well, reserving the marinade.

Fry the halloumi in a nonstick skillet over medium heat until golden brown on both sides. Remove and set aside.

Add the cherry and teardrop tomatoes to the skillet and cook until the skins burst. Heat the reserved marinade and add to the cooked tomatoes.

Dip the green tomato slices into the buttermilk, then coat in the polenta.

Heat the vegetable oil in a large nonstick skillet and panfry the coated tomato slices over medium heat until brown. Drain on paper towels. Serve the halloumi on a bed of arugula topped with tomatoes and drizzled with the reserved marinade. Sprinkle with marjoram leaves.

SERVES 4

sweet potato and bell pepper rosti with pork sausages

2 red bell peppers
1 lb boiling potatoes, unpeeled
¾ lb orange sweet potatoes, peeled
1 onion, grated
2 tablespoons chopped cilantro leaves
3 tablespoons olive oil
8 pork sausages
2 handfuls arugula
3½ oz crumbled feta cheese

Broil the bell peppers on high heat until the skins blister. Place in a plastic bag and allow to cool. Remove peels and cut into strips.

Boil or steam the boiling potatoes and sweet potatoes until tender. Allow to cool slightly, then grate into a bowl. Add the onion, bell pepper, and cilantro.

Heat half of the oil in a large nonstick skillet, spread the mixture evenly over the base of the skillet, and cook over medium heat for 10 minutes, or until the base is crisp and golden. Slide the rosti onto a plate, add the remaining oil to the skillet, then flip the rosti back into the skillet and cook for an additional 8 minutes. Remove and keep warm.

Fry the sausages until tender, then cut into thick slices. Cut the rosti into wedges and serve topped with arugula, sausages, and crumbled feta.

SERVES 4–6

corn fritters with crispy prosciutto

8 ripe plum tomatoes, halved
sea salt and freshly ground black pepper, to taste
1/2 cup spicy tomato chutney
1 1/2 cups self-rising flour
1/2 cup coarse polenta
1 teaspoon sugar
1 egg, lightly beaten
1 1/2 cups buttermilk
2 ears corn, kernels removed,
    or 14 oz canned corn kernels, drained
4 scallions, chopped
2 tablespoons snipped chives
1/4 cup grated Parmesan cheese
4 tablespoons olive oil
12 thin slices prosciutto
chervil leaves, to serve

Preheat the oven to 400°F. Place the tomatoes on a nonstick baking sheet, sprinkle with salt and pepper, and bake for 30 minutes, or until tender. Chop and combine with the chutney.

Sift the flour, polenta, and sugar into a large bowl, and whisk in the combined egg and buttermilk until smooth. Fold in the corn, scallions, chives, and Parmesan. Season with sea salt and freshly ground black pepper.

Heat the oil in a nonstick skillet, and spoon 3 tablespoons of the corn mixture into the skillet. Cook for 2 minutes over medium heat. Turn and cook until golden. Repeat with the remaining mixture. Broil the prosciutto until crisp. Serve the fritters with the tomato chutney, prosciutto, and chervil.

SERVES 4

smoked ham, egg, and jarlsberg cheese sandwiches

1 unsliced loaf white bread, cut into eight ¾-inch-thick slices
3 tablespoons Dijon mustard
1 tablespoon oil
4 eggs
2 cups finely sliced or shaved honey-smoked ham
1 cup shaved Jarlsberg or Swiss cheese
¼ cup butter, softened

Spread one side of each slice of bread with the Dijon mustard.

Heat the oil in a nonstick skillet, add the eggs, and fry until cooked as desired (soft in the center works best). Top four of the slices of bread with some shaved ham, an egg, and the cheese, then place the lids on top.

Butter the outside of each sandwich, top and bottom. Heat a skillet over medium heat, and cook the sandwiches in batches, with a plate on top of them to weigh them down, until crisp and golden on both sides. You will know they are ready when the cheese starts melting and oozing out of the sides. Serve immediately.

SERVES 4

NOTE: These sandwiches also work well when made in a sandwich maker.

eggs benedict

HOLLANDAISE SAUCE
3/4 cup butter
4 egg yolks
1 teaspoon tarragon vinegar

4 thick slices rye bread
8 slices ham
1 tablespoon white vinegar
8 eggs
freshly ground black pepper, to taste

To make the hollandaise, melt the butter in a small saucepan. Place the egg yolks, the tarragon vinegar, and 2 tablespoons water in a food processor and, with the motor running, gradually add the butter. Process until thick and creamy.

Toast the bread on both sides and top with the sliced ham.

Half-fill a deep skillet with water, bring to a slow simmer, and add the white vinegar. One by one, break the eggs onto a plate and slide them into the skillet. Cook for 3 minutes, or until done as desired.

Top each piece of toast and ham with two poached eggs, and drizzle with the hollandaise sauce. Sprinkle with pepper.

SERVES 4

cheese and herb corn bread with scrambled eggs

CORN BREAD

1¼ cups self-rising flour

1 tablespoon superfine sugar

2 teaspoons baking powder

1 teaspoon sea salt

¾ cup fine polenta

½ cup grated cheddar cheese

1 handful chopped mixed herbs (such as chives, dill, parsley)

2 eggs

1 cup buttermilk

4 tablespoons macadamia or olive oil

SCRAMBLED EGGS

6 eggs

½ cup whipping cream

sea salt and freshly ground black pepper, to taste

small basil leaves, to garnish

Preheat the oven to 350°F. Grease an 8 inch x 4 inch loaf pan. Sift the flour, sugar, baking powder, and salt into a bowl. Add the polenta, cheese, herbs, eggs, buttermilk, and oil, and mix to combine. Spoon the mixture into the loaf pan and bake for 45 minutes, or until a skewer comes out clean when inserted into the bread. Remove from the pan.

To make the scrambled eggs, whisk together the eggs and cream, then season. Pour the mixture into a nonstick skillet and cook over low heat, stirring until the egg is just set. Serve the scrambled eggs with slices of buttered corn bread. Sprinkle with basil leaves.

SERVES 4

bagels with smoked salmon and caper salsa

4 plain or rye bagels
½ cup Neufchatel cheese
8 oz sliced smoked salmon
2 scallions, chopped
2 plum tomatoes, finely chopped
2 tablespoons baby capers, rinsed and drained
2 tablespoons finely chopped dill
2 tablespoons lemon juice
1 tablespoon extra-virgin olive oil

Cut the bagels in half and spread the base generously with the cheese, then top with the salmon.

Combine the scallions, tomatoes, capers, dill, lemon juice, and olive oil in a bowl. Pile this mixture onto the salmon and serve.

SERVES 4

whitebait with crème fraîche tartar sauce

1 lb whitebait
1 cup all-purpose flour
sea salt and freshly ground black pepper, to taste
vegetable oil, for deep-frying

TARTAR SAUCE
¾ cup crème fraîche or sour cream
2 tablespoons mayonnaise
3 pickles, finely chopped
2 tablespoons capers, rinsed, drained, and finely chopped
1 teaspoon lemon juice
1 tablespoon chopped Italian parsley

Rinse the whitebait and pat dry. Place the flour in a bowl and season with salt and pepper. Toss the whitebait in the flour, shaking off any excess.

Heat the oil in a deep skillet until a cube of bread browns in 15 seconds when dropped into it. Cook the whitebait, in batches, for 1–2 minutes, or until crisp and golden. Remove and drain on paper towels.

To make the tartar sauce, combine the crème fraîche, mayonnaise, pickles, capers, lemon juice, and parsley in a bowl. Serve piles of the fried whitebait on plates, accompanied with a small bowl of tartar sauce.

SERVES 4

savory

crispy lavash tiles with butter mushrooms

3 pieces pita bread
2 tablespoons olive oil
¼ cup finely grated Parmesan cheese
¼ cup plus 2 tablespoons butter
4 scallions, sliced
1¾ lb mixed mushrooms (portobello, white
    button, cremini, matsutake, enoki), sliced
1 tablespoon chervil leaves

Preheat the oven to 350°F. Cut the pita bread into 1¼-inch-wide strips and brush lightly with 1 tablespoon of the oil. Sprinkle with the Parmesan cheese and bake for 10 minutes, or until crispy.

Heat the butter and the remaining oil in a large skillet until sizzling. Add the scallions and the portobello mushrooms, and cook over medium heat until they are tender. Add the button mushrooms, cremini, and matsutake, and cook until the liquid has evaporated. Remove from the heat and stir in the enoki mushrooms.

Arrange the toasted pita strips into an interlocking square. Pile the mushrooms in the center, top with the chervil, and serve immediately.

SERVES 4

individual herbed lemon ricotta

1 lb ricotta cheese
crusty bread, to serve

DRESSING
2 tablespoons olive oil
1 garlic clove, crushed
zest of 1 lemon
2 tablespoons lemon juice
1 tablespoon balsamic vinegar
½ cup olive oil
1 cup roughly chopped sun-dried tomatoes
4 tablespoons chopped Italian parsley

Lightly grease and line four ½-cup ramekins with plastic wrap. Divide the ricotta between the molds and press down firmly. Cover with plastic wrap and refrigerate for 2 hours.

Preheat the oven to 425°F. Unmold the ricottas onto a baking sheet lined with baking paper, and bake for 20 minutes, or until golden.

To make the dressing, combine all the ingredients in a bowl.

Place each baked ricotta into a shallow bowl and pour a little of the dressing over each one. Serve immediately with crusty bread.

SERVES 4

caramelized leek, goat cheese, and spinach pie

PIECRUST
2 cups all-purpose flour
1/2 cup butter

FILLING
2 tablespoons olive oil
1 leek, thinly sliced
1 head fennel, thinly sliced
1/3 lb baby spinach leaves
2/3 cup crumbled goat cheese
3 eggs, lightly beaten
2/3 cup whipping cream

Preheat the oven to 400°F. Place the flour and butter in a food processor and process until the mixture resembles bread crumbs. Gradually add 3–4 tablespoons iced water until the dough comes together. Gather into a ball, cover with plastic wrap, and refrigerate for 20 minutes.

Roll the piecrust out on a floured surface to fit an 8-inch fluted pie pan. Ease into the pan and trim off the excess dough. Line with baking paper and fill with baking weights or rice. Bake for 15 minutes, then remove the weights and paper and bake for another 10 minutes. Reduce the oven to 315°F.

Heat the oil in a skillet over medium heat, add the leek and fennel, and cook for 20 minutes. Remove. Add the spinach and cook until wilted. Spread the leek and fennel over the piecrust. Top with the spinach and cheese. Combine the eggs and cream, pour into the piecrust, and bake for 40 minutes.

SERVES 6

twice-baked cheese soufflés

1 cup milk
3 black peppercorns
1 onion, cut in half and studded with 2 cloves
1 bay leaf
¼ cup butter
¼ cup self-rising flour
2 eggs, separated
1 cup grated Gruyère cheese
1 cup whipping cream
½ cup finely grated Parmesan cheese

Preheat the oven to 350°F. Lightly grease four ½-cup ramekins. Place the milk, peppercorns, onion, and bay leaf in a saucepan, and heat until almost boiling. Remove from the heat and allow to infuse for 10 minutes. Strain.

Melt the butter in a saucepan, add the flour, and cook over medium heat for 1 minute. Remove from the heat and stir in the infused milk, then return to the heat and stir until the mixture thickens. Simmer for 1 minute.

Transfer the mixture to a bowl and add the egg yolks and Gruyère cheese. Beat the egg whites until soft peaks form, then gently fold into the cheese sauce. Divide the mixture between the ramekins and place in a baking pan half-filled with hot water. Bake for 15 minutes. Remove from the baking pan, cool, and refrigerate. Preheat the oven to 400°F. Remove the soufflés from the ramekins and place onto ovenproof plates. Pour the cream over the top and sprinkle with Parmesan. Bake for 20 minutes, or until puffed and golden.

SERVES 4

potato flowers with salmon, asparagus, and quail eggs

DRESSING
¼ cup mayonnaise
2 tablespoons plain yogurt
2 garlic cloves, crushed
1 tablespoon lime juice

½ cup butter
4 potatoes, peeled and cut into paper-thin slices
sea salt, to season
24 asparagus spears
8 quail eggs
7 oz gravlax slices (see page 49 for instructions on
    making gravlax at home)
freshly ground black pepper, to taste

Place all the dressing ingredients in a bowl and whisk to combine. Preheat the oven to 475°F. Melt the butter in a small saucepan. Spoon off any froth that settles on top, and carefully pour off the yellow butter, discarding the milky sediment in the bottom of the pan. Pour half of the butter onto a baking sheet. Toss the potato slices in salt, then place four potato slices about 6 inches apart onto the sheet. Arrange the remaining slices around them, overlapping to form eight flowers. Brush with a little more butter. Bake for 8 minutes, or until the edges are brown, then turn and cook for an additional 3 minutes, or until cooked through. Steam the asparagus spears until tender.

Heat the remaining butter in a nonstick skillet. Crack the quail eggs using a knife, and cook over low heat for 1–2 minutes, or until the whites have set. Serve two potato flowers on each plate, topped with the asparagus, slices of gravlax, two quail eggs, and the dressing. Season with pepper.

mushrooms with marinated feta

20 asparagus spears
10 oz marinated feta cheese
3 tablespoons extra-virgin olive oil
zest of 1 lemon
2 garlic cloves, crushed
2 tablespoons lemon juice
freshly ground black pepper, to taste
4 large portobello mushrooms, stems removed
2 large tomatoes, cut into thick slices
4 eggs
oregano leaves, to serve

Trim the ends from the asparagus.

Drain the oil from the feta and place in a nonmetallic bowl. Stir in the olive oil, lemon zest, garlic, and lemon juice. Season with pepper.

Place the mushrooms and tomatoes in a shallow dish and pour the oil mixture over them. Toss gently to coat, then let marinate for 15 minutes. Drain the mushrooms, reserving the marinade, and cook together with the tomatoes on a lightly oiled grill plate until tender. Add the asparagus toward the end of cooking, and add the eggs last.

Place the mushrooms on a plate, top each one with some asparagus spears, a slice of tomato, an egg, and some sliced feta. Drizzle with the oil marinade and top with oregano.

SERVES 4

squiggly corn crab cakes

3½ oz corn spaghetti

18 oz fresh or canned crabmeat

1 small red bell pepper, finely chopped

1 tablespoon capers, rinsed, drained, and roughly chopped

2 tablespoons lime juice

1 teaspoon grated lime zest

1 teaspoon Tabasco sauce

6 scallions, chopped

1 egg, lightly beaten

1½ cups fresh bread crumbs

peanut oil, for panfrying

chili jelly, to serve

Cook the pasta in a large saucepan of rapidly boiling water until al dente. Drain well and lay out to dry on paper towels, then cut into short lengths.

Combine the pasta, crabmeat, bell pepper, capers, lime juice, lime zest, Tabasco, scallions, egg, and bread crumbs. Divide the mixture into eight equal portions and shape into patties. Place on a tray and refrigerate for 30 minutes.

Heat the oil in a large, deep skillet to 350°F, or until a cube of bread browns in 15 seconds when dropped into the oil. Panfry the crab cakes in batches for 3 minutes on each side, or until crisp and golden brown. Serve with chili jelly.

SERVES 4

gravlax with parmesan sheets

1 five-lb whole salmon, filleted
1 cup finely chopped dill
3/4 cup sea salt
1/3 cup sugar
1 tablespoon white peppercorns, finely crushed
2 cups finely grated Parmesan cheese
sour cream, to serve
chervil, to serve
freshly ground black pepper, to taste

Place one salmon fillet, skin side down, in a large, shallow, nonmetallic dish. Combine the dill, salt, sugar, and crushed peppercorns, and spread this mixture over the length of the fillet. Place the second salmon fillet on top, skin side up. Cover with plastic wrap and weigh down with a cutting board and some heavy cans. Refrigerate for two days, turning the salmon as a whole piece every 12 hours and pouring off any excess liquid. When marinated, cut the salmon into wafer-thin slices.

To make the Parmesan sheets, preheat the oven to 350°F. Thinly sprinkle the Parmesan into 3-inch triangle shapes (to make at least one per serving) onto two baking sheets lined with baking paper. Bake for 10 minutes, or until crisp. Top with gravlax, sour cream, chervil, and black pepper.

SERVES 10–12

bruschetta with
salmon tartare and roe

1 loaf crusty bread, cut into ½-inch-thick slices

3 garlic cloves, cut in half

extra-virgin olive oil, for brushing, plus
    2 tablespoons for marinade

18 oz skinless salmon fillets

2 tablespoons snipped chives

2 tablespoons lime juice

sea salt and freshly ground black pepper, to taste

⅓ cup crème fraîche

3 heaping tablespoons salmon roe

Toast both sides of the bread until golden, then rub one side of each slice with the halved garlic cloves and brush generously with the extra-virgin olive oil.

Cut the salmon fillets into ½-inch dice, place in a nonmetallic bowl with the chives, lime juice, and 2 tablespoons extra olive oil, and season with salt and cracked black pepper. Serve the salmon tartare immediately on the slices of bruschetta, topped with a small spoonful each of crème fraîche and salmon roe.

SERVES 6

arugula, mushroom, and blue cheese omelet

3 tablespoons butter
3¼ oz portobello mushrooms, sliced
1 garlic clove, crushed
3 eggs, separated
sea salt and freshly ground black pepper, to taste
½ cup finely grated Parmesan cheese
1 handful finely shredded arugula
⅓ cup crumbled creamy blue cheese

Heat 1 tablespoon of the butter in a nonstick skillet. Brown the mushrooms and garlic over high heat for 5 minutes. Remove from the skillet.

Whisk the egg whites in a dry bowl until stiff peaks form. Whisk the egg yolks in a separate bowl and season well with salt and pepper. Fold the egg whites into the yolks with a large metal spoon, then fold through all but 1 tablespoon of the Parmesan along with the mushrooms and arugula.

Heat the remaining butter in the skillet until foaming. Pour the egg mixture into the skillet and cook over medium heat for 1–2 minutes, or until the omelet starts to come away from the side of the skillet.

Sprinkle with the blue cheese and cook under a hot broiler until just set. Fold the omelet over and slide onto a plate. Top with the reserved Parmesan.

SERVES 1

savory

fried halloumi, tomato, and arugula sandwiches

1 lb halloumi cheese, thickly sliced
1 tablespoon finely shredded preserved lemon, or
    finely shredded fresh lemon zest
2 garlic cloves, crushed
1 tablespoon roughly chopped capers, rinsed and squeezed dry
1 tablespoon extra-virgin olive oil
8 thick slices sourdough bread
4 tomatoes, thickly sliced
1 handful arugula
sea salt and freshly ground black pepper, to taste
1/4 cup butter

Put the halloumi in a nonmetallic dish. Whisk together the lemon, garlic, capers, and olive oil, and pour over the halloumi. Toss well, then divide the cheese among four slices of bread. Top with the tomatoes and arugula, and season generously with salt and pepper. Sandwich with the rest of the bread.

Melt the butter in a large skillet and cook the sandwiches over medium heat until the bread is crisp and the cheese is soft. Serve immediately.

SERVES 4

scrambled eggs and salmon on croissants

4 eggs
4 tablespoons whipping cream
sea salt and freshly ground black pepper, to taste
3 tablespoons unsalted butter
4½ oz smoked salmon, sliced
2 teaspoons finely chopped dill
2 croissants or 2 individual brioche buns

Beat the eggs and cream together in a bowl. Season with salt and freshly ground black pepper.

Melt the butter in a nonstick skillet over low heat, then add the eggs. Using a flat-ended wooden spoon, push the mixture around until it starts to set, then add the salmon and dill. Continue to cook, gently folding the salmon and dill through the mixture until the eggs are mostly cooked and there is just a little liquid left in the pan.

Serve the croissants filled with the scrambled eggs.

SERVES 2

mini savory breakfast pies

1¾ cups all-purpose flour
½ teaspoon salt
½ cup plus 1 tablespoon butter, diced
4 slices ham
2 tablespoons chopped Italian parsley
2 tomatoes, finely chopped
8 eggs
½ cup whipping cream
4 tablespoons grated Parmesan cheese
sea salt and freshly ground black pepper, to taste

Preheat the oven to 400°F. Sift the flour and ½ teaspoon salt into a food processor, add the butter, and process for a few seconds until the mixture resembles bread crumbs. Bring the dough together using your hands, and shape into a ball. Wrap the ball in plastic wrap, flatten slightly, and put in the refrigerator for 10 minutes.

Roll the piecrust out on a floured work surface until it is very thin. Cut out four 6¼-inch circles and use them to line four 4-inch tartlet pans. Press the piecrust gently into the flutes of the pans. Line each pan with a piece of crumpled waxed paper and some uncooked rice. Bake the piecrust for 10 minutes, then take out the paper and rice and bake for an additional minute.

Line each piecrust base with the ham (you may need to cut it into pieces to make it fit neatly). Sprinkle with the parsley and add the tomato. Gently break two eggs into each pan, then pour a quarter of the cream over the top of each, sprinkle with Parmesan, and season with salt and pepper.

Bake the pies for 15–20 minutes, or until the egg whites are set. Serve hot.

SERVES 4

cheese and onion waffles with herbed ricotta and roasted tomato

4 plum tomatoes, halved
1 tablespoon olive oil
1 tablespoon balsamic vinegar
1 teaspoon sugar
1 tablespoon chopped oregano
1¼ cups ricotta cheese
4 tablespoons chopped herbs (oregano, sage, rosemary, parsley)
sea salt and freshly ground black pepper, to taste
1½ cups self-rising flour
3 tablespoons freshly grated Parmesan cheese
3 tablespoons grated cheddar cheese
3 large scallions, finely chopped
1 egg
1 cup milk
2 egg whites

Preheat the oven to 315°F. Lightly grease a baking sheet. Place the tomato halves on the sheet and drizzle with olive oil and balsamic vinegar. Sprinkle with the sugar, oregano, and salt. Bake for 1 hour, or until soft.

Put the ricotta in a bowl and fold in the chopped herbs. Season with salt and pepper. Divide the herbed ricotta mixture into four even portions and refrigerate.

Place the flour, Parmesan, cheddar, scallion, whole egg, and milk in a bowl. Season with salt and pepper, then mix well. Whisk the egg whites, then fold them into the cheese and egg mixture. Preheat a waffle iron and brush with olive oil. Pour in ⅓ cup waffle batter and cook until golden on both sides. To serve, top the waffles with the tomato halves and ricotta mixture.

savory

SERVES 4

french toast with crispy prosciutto

3 tablespoons whipping cream
3 eggs
3 tablespoons superfine sugar
pinch cinnamon
8 thick slices bread, cut in half diagonally
¼ cup plus 1 tablespoon butter
1 tablespoon olive oil
12 slices prosciutto
maple syrup, to serve (optional)

Combine the cream, eggs, sugar, and cinnamon in a wide, shallow bowl and mix together. Soak the bread in the egg mixture, one slice at a time, shaking off any excess.

Melt half the butter in a skillet, add 3 or 4 slices of bread in a single layer, and cook until golden brown on both sides. Cook the remaining bread in batches, adding more butter as needed, and keeping the cooked slices warm in the oven.

Heat the olive oil in a skillet, add the prosciutto, and fry until crisp. Remove and drain on paper towels. Place the prosciutto on top of the French toast and serve. Drizzle with maple syrup, if using.

SERVES 4

fried eggs and tomatoes on scallion potato cakes

2/3 lb all-purpose potatoes, peeled and roughly chopped
1 egg yolk
1/2 cup grated cheddar cheese
3 scallions, finely chopped
2 tablespoons finely chopped Italian parsley
sea salt and freshly ground black pepper, to taste
1 tablespoon all-purpose flour
4 tablespoons olive oil
1 garlic clove, sliced
3–4 plum tomatoes, halved lengthwise
butter, for frying
4 eggs

Boil the potatoes in a saucepan of salted water until tender. Drain, then mash the potatoes. Stir in the egg yolk, cheddar, scallions, and parsley, and season with salt and pepper. Form into four patties. Tip the flour onto a plate and coat the patties with it. Cover and chill for 30 minutes.

Heat 1 tablespoon of the oil in a large skillet over medium heat. Fry the patties for 4–5 minutes on both sides, or until golden brown. Keep warm.

Heat 1 tablespoon of the oil in the skillet over low heat. Add the garlic and fry for 2 minutes. Add the tomatoes, cut side down, and fry for 10–15 minutes, turning them once during cooking.

Heat a heavy-based nonstick skillet over medium heat and add the remaining oil and a little butter. Fry the eggs for about 1 minute. Serve the eggs with the scallion potato cakes and tomatoes.

SERVES 2–4

savory

broiled field mushrooms with garlic and chili

3 tablespoons butter, softened
1 garlic clove, crushed
1–2 small red chilies, finely chopped
4 tablespoons finely chopped Italian parsley
4 large or 8 medium portobello mushrooms
sea salt and freshly ground black pepper, to taste
4 thick slices ciabatta bread
tomato chutney or relish, to serve
crème fraîche, to serve

Mix together the butter, garlic, chilies, and parsley, and spread some of the mixture over the inside of each mushroom. Season well with salt and pepper.

Heat the broiler to medium and line the base of the broiler tray with foil. Broil the mushrooms for about 8 minutes, or until cooked through.

Toast the bread, spread some tomato chutney or relish on each slice, then top with a mushroom (or two) and serve immediately with a dollop of crème fraîche.

SERVES 4

piperade

2 tablespoons olive oil
1 large onion, thinly sliced
2 red bell peppers, cut into batons
2 garlic cloves, crushed
1½ lb tomatoes
pinch cayenne pepper
sea salt and freshly ground black pepper, to taste
8 eggs, lightly beaten
1½ tablespoons butter
4 thin slices ham

Heat the oil in a large heavy-based skillet over medium heat, then add the onion. Cook for about 3 minutes, or until soft. Add the bell pepper and garlic, cover, and cook for 8 minutes, stirring frequently.

Score a cross in the base of each tomato. Put in a large bowl of boiling water for 20 seconds, then drain and plunge into a bowl of cold water. Remove the tomatoes and peel the skin away from the cross. Chop the flesh and discard the cores. Add the chopped tomato and cayenne to the bell pepper mixture, cover the skillet, and cook for an additional 5 minutes.

Uncover the skillet and increase the heat. Cook for 3 minutes, or until the juices have evaporated, shaking the skillet often. Season well with salt and freshly ground black pepper.

Add the eggs and scramble into the mixture until fully cooked.

Heat the butter in a small skillet over medium heat and fry the ham. Arrange the piperade on four plates, top with the cooked ham, and serve with buttered toast.

SERVES 4

mushroom omelet with chorizo

¼ cup butter
1 chorizo sausage, sliced
3½ oz mushrooms, thinly sliced
6 eggs
sea salt and freshly ground black pepper, to taste
2 tablespoons chives, finely chopped

Heat 2 tablespoons of the butter in a small omelet pan or skillet over medium heat. Add the chorizo and fry for about 5 minutes, or until golden, then remove it from the skillet using a slotted spoon. Add the mushrooms to the skillet and cook, stirring frequently, for about 4 minutes, or until soft. Add to the chorizo.

Break the eggs into a bowl and season with salt and freshly ground black pepper. Add the chives and beat lightly with a fork.

Melt half the remaining butter in the skillet over medium heat, add half the eggs, and cook for 20 seconds, then quickly stir the mixture with a fork. Work quickly, drawing away some of the cooked egg from the bottom of the skillet and allowing some of the uncooked egg to set, tilting the skillet a little as you go. Once the eggs are mostly set, arrange half the mushrooms and chorizo on top.

Cook for an additional minute, if necessary. Tip the omelet out onto a plate and keep warm while you cook the second omelet. Serve immediately.

SERVES 2

croque madame

3 eggs
1 tablespoon milk
sea salt and freshly ground black pepper, to taste
2 tablespoons butter, softened
4 slices white bread
1 teaspoon Dijon mustard
4 slices Gruyère cheese
2 slices ham
2 teaspoons oil

Crack 1 egg into a wide shallow bowl, add the milk, and lightly beat. Season with salt and freshly ground black pepper.

Butter the bread using half the butter and spread half the slices with Dijon mustard. Place a slice of cheese on top, then the ham, and then another slice of cheese. Top with the remaining bread.

Heat the remaining butter and the oil in a large nonstick skillet over medium heat. While the butter is melting, dip one sandwich into the egg and milk mixture, coating the bread on both sides. When the butter is sizzling, add the sandwich and cook for 1½ minutes on one side, pressing down firmly with a spatula. Turn over and cook the other side, then move it to the side of the skillet.

Gently break an egg into the skillet and fry until it is done as desired.

Transfer the sandwich to a plate and top with the fried egg. Keep warm while you repeat with the remaining sandwich and egg, adding more butter and oil to the skillet if necessary. Serve immediately.

SERVES 2

savory

huevos rancheros

1½ tablespoons olive oil
1 onion, finely chopped
1 green bell pepper, finely chopped
2 red chilies, finely chopped
1 garlic clove, crushed
½ teaspoon dried oregano
2 tomatoes, chopped
28 oz canned chopped tomatoes
sea salt and freshly ground black pepper, to taste
8 eggs
4 flour tortillas
⅔ cup crumbled feta cheese

Heat the olive oil in a large skillet over medium heat. Add the onion and green bell pepper and fry for 3 minutes, or until soft.

Add the chilies and garlic, stir, and then add the oregano, fresh and canned tomatoes, and ¾ cup water. Bring to a boil, then reduce the heat, cover with a lid, and simmer gently for 8–10 minutes, or until the sauce thickens. Season with salt and pepper.

Smooth the surface of the mixture, then make eight hollows with the back of a spoon. Break an egg into each hollow and put the lid on the skillet. Cook the eggs for 5 minutes, or until they are set.

While the eggs are cooking, heat the tortillas according to the instructions on the package, then cut each into quarters.

Serve the eggs with some feta crumbled over them and the tortillas on the side.

SERVES 4

spanish omelet with smoked salmon

1 tablespoon olive oil
1 lb all-purpose potatoes, peeled and cubed
1 onion, finely chopped
8 eggs
2 tablespoons chopped dill
sea salt and freshly ground black pepper, to taste
8 slices smoked salmon
1/3 cup mascarpone cheese
4 handfuls salad leaves

Heat the oil in a nonstick skillet and add the potato. Fry gently, stirring, for 10 minutes, or until browned on all sides and cooked through.

Add the onion to the skillet and cook for 2–3 minutes, or until translucent and soft. Heat the broiler to medium.

Whisk the eggs in a bowl together with the dill and some salt and freshly ground black pepper.

Tear the smoked salmon into pieces and add to the skillet. Add the mascarpone in dollops. Using a spatula, pull the mixture into the center of the skillet and level it off.

Pour the eggs over the top and cook for 5–10 minutes, or until the omelet is just set.

Put the skillet under the broiler for 1–2 minutes to lightly brown the top. Slide the omelet out of the skillet and cut into eight wedges. Arrange a handful of salad leaves on each plate and top with two wedges of omelet.

SERVES 4

savory

fried egg and red onion wrap

1½ tablespoons olive oil

3 red onions, thickly sliced

1 large red bell pepper, sliced

3 tablespoons balsamic vinegar

4 eggs

4 pieces lavash or other unleavened bread

4 tablespoons sour cream

sweet chili sauce, to serve

sea salt and freshly ground black pepper, to taste

Heat the olive oil in a nonstick skillet over medium heat and add the onions. Cook, stirring occasionally, until soft and translucent. Add the bell pepper and cook until soft. Increase the heat and stir for 1–2 minutes, or until they start to brown, then stir in the balsamic vinegar. Remove the mixture from the skillet and keep warm.

Carefully break the eggs into the skillet and, keeping them separate, cook over low heat until they are just set.

Heat the lavash under a broiler for a few seconds. Spread 1 tablespoon of sour cream onto the center of each piece of bread, then drizzle with some of the sweet chili sauce. Top with the onion and bell pepper mixture and an egg. Season with salt and pepper.

Fold in one short end of each piece of lavash, then roll up each one lengthwise.

SERVES 4

salmon and dill potato patties with lime mayonnaise

1 lb new potatoes, cut in half

2 teaspoons grated lime zest

1¼ cups mayonnaise

15 oz canned salmon, drained, bones removed

1 tablespoon chopped dill

2 scallions, thinly sliced

sea salt and freshly ground black pepper, to taste

1 egg

1 cup fresh bread crumbs

3 tablespoons oil

4 handfuls arugula

lime wedges, to serve

Cook the potatoes in a large saucepan of boiling water for 12–15 minutes, or until tender. Drain well and cool.

Combine the lime zest and 1 cup of the mayonnaise.

Transfer the potatoes to a large bowl, then mash roughly with the back of a spoon, leaving some large chunks. Stir in the salmon, dill, and scallions, and season with salt and pepper. Mix in the egg and the remaining mayonnaise. Divide into eight portions, forming palm-size patties. Press lightly into the bread crumbs to coat.

Heat the oil in a nonstick skillet over medium heat and cook the patties, turning, for 3–4 minutes, or until golden brown. Drain on paper towels. Serve with a dollop of lime mayonnaise, arugula leaves, and lime wedges.

SERVES 4

savory

classic omelet

12 eggs
sea salt and freshly ground black pepper, to taste
4 tablespoons butter

Beat the eggs in a bowl with ⅔ cup water and season with salt and freshly ground black pepper.

Heat 1 tablespoon of the butter in a small skillet or omelet pan over high heat. When the butter is foaming, reduce the heat to medium and add one-quarter of the egg mixture. Tilt the skillet to cover the base with the egg and leave for a few seconds. Using a spatula, draw the sides of the omelet into the center and let any extra liquid egg run to the edges.

If you are adding a filling to the omelet, sprinkle it over the egg. As soon as the egg is almost set, use an egg slide to fold the omelet in half in the skillet. It should still be soft inside. Slide it onto a warm serving plate and repeat to make three more omelets.

SERVES 4

FILLINGS

Sprinkle each omelet with ⅓ cup roughly torn arugula and ⅓ cup crumbled goat cheese.

Sauté ½ lb finely sliced white button mushrooms in ¼ cup butter, add 4 tablespoons finely chopped basil, and sprinkle over the omelet.

herbed garlic mushrooms with goat cheese bruschetta

1/4 cup plus 1 tablespoon butter

4 garlic cloves, crushed

2/3 cup chopped Italian parsley

4 large portobello mushrooms, stalks removed

4 large slices crusty bread

2 tablespoons olive oil

5 1/2 oz goat cheese, at room temperature

1 handful baby arugula

freshly ground black pepper, to taste

Preheat the oven to 350°F. Melt the butter in a small saucepan, add the garlic and parsley, and cook, stirring, for 1 minute, or until well combined. Spoon the mixture evenly over the underside of the mushrooms. Line a baking sheet with baking paper. Place the mushrooms on the sheet, filling side up, and cover with foil. Bake for 20 minutes, or until softened and cooked through.

Brush both sides of the bread with the olive oil, then broil until crisp and golden brown.

Spread the bruschetta with the softened goat cheese and top with the arugula. Cut the garlic mushrooms in half and place two halves on each bruschetta, then drizzle with the cooking juices and season with ground black pepper. Serve immediately.

SERVES 4

mini sweet potato and leek frittatas

1 lb orange sweet potatoes
1 tablespoon olive oil
1 tablespoon butter
2 leeks, white part only, thinly sliced
1 garlic clove, crushed
3/4 cup crumbled feta cheese
8 eggs
1/2 cup whipping cream
sea salt and freshly ground black pepper, to taste
arugula, to serve (optional)

Preheat the oven to 350°F. Grease a twelve-hole muffin pan. Cut small rounds of baking paper and place into the base of each hole. Cut the sweet potatoes into small cubes and steam until tender. Drain well and set aside.

Heat the oil and butter in a large skillet, add the leek, and cook for 10 minutes, stirring occasionally, or until very soft and lightly golden. Add the garlic and cook for an additional minute. Cool, then stir in the feta and sweet potato. Divide the mixture evenly among the muffin holes.

Whisk the eggs and cream together and season with salt and freshly ground black pepper. Pour the egg mixture into each hole until three-quarters filled, then press the vegetables down gently. Bake for 25–30 minutes, or until golden and set. Leave in the holes for 5 minutes, then ease out with a knife and cool on a wire rack before serving with arugula.

MAKES 12 FRITTATAS

potato tortilla

1 lb potatoes, cut into ½-inch slices
3 tablespoons olive oil
1 onion, thinly sliced
4 garlic cloves, thinly sliced
2 tablespoons finely chopped Italian parsley
6 eggs
1 teaspoon sea salt
1 teaspoon freshly ground black pepper

Place the potato slices in a large saucepan, cover with cold water, and bring to a boil over high heat. Boil for 5 minutes, then drain and set aside.

Heat the oil in a deep-sided nonstick skillet over medium heat. Add the onion and garlic and cook for 5 minutes, or until the onion softens.

Add the potatoes and parsley to the skillet and stir to combine. Cook over medium heat for 5 minutes, gently pressing down into the skillet.

Whisk the eggs with the salt and freshly ground black pepper, and pour evenly over the potatoes. Cover and cook over medium heat for about 20 minutes, or until the egg is just set. Cut into wedges to serve.

SERVES 6–8

savory

kedgeree

12 oz undyed smoked haddock
3 slices lemon
1 bay leaf
1¼ cups milk
1 cup long-grain rice
¼ cup butter
1 small onion, finely chopped
2 teaspoons mild curry powder
1 tablespoon finely chopped Italian parsley
3 eggs, hard-boiled, roughly chopped
⅔ cup heavy cream
freshly ground black pepper, to taste
mango chutney, to serve

Put the smoked haddock in a deep skillet with the lemon and bay leaf, cover with the milk, and simmer for 6 minutes, or until cooked through. Remove the fish and break into large flakes. Discard any bones.

Put the rice in a saucepan along with 1⅓ cups water, bring to a boil, cover, and cook for 10 minutes, or until just cooked. Drain any excess water and fork through to fluff up the rice.

Melt the butter in a skillet over medium heat. Add the onion and cook for 3 minutes, or until soft. Add the curry powder and cook for an additional 2 minutes. Add the rice and stir through, cooking for 2–3 minutes, or until heated through. Add the fish, parsley, eggs, and cream, and stir until heated through. Season with pepper and serve with mango chutney.

SERVES 4

apricot and bran breakfast shake

½ cup dried apricots
1 tablespoon oat bran
1 tablespoon honey
3 tablespoons apricot yogurt
2½ cups milk

Pour enough boiling water over the dried apricots to cover them, then leave until they are plump and rehydrated. Drain well.

Place the apricots, oat bran, honey, yogurt, and milk in a blender, and mix until thick and smooth. Divide among glasses and serve.

SERVES 2–4

creamy and rich banana and macadamia smoothie

2 bananas, slightly frozen
1/2 cup honey-roasted macadamia nuts
2 tablespoons vanilla yogurt
2 tablespoons wheat germ
2 cups milk
1 banana, extra, cut in half lengthwise

Place the frozen bananas, two-thirds of the macadamia nuts, the yogurt, the wheat germ, and the milk in a blender, and whizz for several minutes until thick and creamy.

Finely chop the remaining macadamias and put on a plate. Toss the banana halves in the nuts to coat.

Stand a banana half in each glass and then pour in the smoothie.

SERVES 2

pandoro with poached peaches and mascarpone

1 cup sugar

3 cardamom pods, bruised

1 bay leaf, plus additional leaves for garnish

1 vanilla bean, split

juice of 1 lemon

6 freestone peaches

4 baby pandoros, cut into thick slices, or 1 baby panettone, sliced

2 eggs, lightly beaten

2 cups milk

¼ cup butter

¾ cup mascarpone cheese or sour cream

3 tablespoons soft brown sugar

Place the sugar, 4 cups of water, the cardamom pods, 1 bay leaf, the vanilla bean, and the lemon juice into a large saucepan and stir over low heat until the sugar dissolves. Bring to a boil and add the peaches. Reduce the heat and simmer for 10 minutes. Remove the peaches, peel, and halve. Boil the syrup until reduced by a third.

Dip the pandoro or panettone into the combined egg and milk mixture. Heat the butter in a large skillet and cook the pandoro or panettone in batches over medium heat until golden brown on both sides.

Combine the mascarpone and brown sugar. Arrange the pandoro or panettone slices on plates, top with the mascarpone mixture and peaches, and drizzle with the syrup. Garnish each plate with a bay leaf.

SERVES 4

maple yogurt balls with sugary balsamic pears

4 cups yogurt

1/2 cup maple syrup

1 tablespoon ground cinnamon

2 tablespoons superfine sugar

1 2/3 cups toasted and roughly chopped hazelnuts

2/3 cup butter

1/2 cup soft brown sugar

3 tablespoons balsamic vinegar

3 small Bosc pears, sliced lengthwise

Combine the yogurt and maple syrup, place onto a large square of doubled cheesecloth, gather the cheesecloth together, and tie tightly with string. Loop the string around a chopstick and suspend over a bowl in the refrigerator for four days to remove any liquid.

Form 1 tablespoon of the yogurt mixture into a ball with moistened hands, and roll the ball in the combined cinnamon and sugar. Then toss in the chopped hazelnuts to coat. Repeat with the remaining yogurt mixture.

Heat the butter in a large skillet, add the brown sugar, and stir over low heat until the sugar dissolves. Stir in the balsamic vinegar and bring the mixture to a boil. Add the pears and simmer until browned on both sides and slightly soft. Arrange on serving plates and top with the yogurt balls.

SERVES 4

healthy nut and seed granola

3⅓ cups puffed corn
1½ cups rolled oats
1 cup pecans
1 cup macadamia nuts, roughly chopped
2 cups flaked coconut
⅓ cup linseeds
⅓ cup sunflower seeds
⅓ cup chopped almonds
1 cup dried apples, chopped
1 cup dried apricots, chopped
⅔ cup dried pears, chopped
½ cup maple syrup
1 teaspoon natural vanilla extract

Preheat the oven to 350°F. Place the puffed corn, rolled oats, pecans, macadamia nuts, coconut, linseeds, sunflower seeds, almonds, apples, apricots, and pears in a bowl, and mix to combine.

Place the maple syrup and vanilla extract in a small saucepan and cook over low heat for 3 minutes, or until the maple syrup becomes easy to pour.

Pour the maple syrup over the nut mixture and toss lightly to coat.

Divide the granola mixture between two nonstick baking dishes. Bake for about 20 minutes, turning frequently, until the granola is lightly toasted. Allow the mixture to cool before transferring it to an airtight container.

MAKES 2½ LB

sweet

cinnamon oatmeal with caramel figs and cream

2 cups rolled oats
1/4 teaspoon ground cinnamon
1/4 cup butter
1/2 cup soft brown sugar
1 1/4 cups whipping cream
6 figs, halved
milk, to serve
1/2 cup heavy cream, to serve

Place the oats, 4 cups of water, and the cinnamon in a saucepan and stir over medium heat for 5 minutes, or until the oatmeal becomes thick and smooth. Set the oatmeal aside.

Melt the butter in a large skillet, add all but 2 tablespoons of the brown sugar, and stir until the sugar dissolves. Stir in the whipping cream and bring the mixture to a boil, then simmer for 5 minutes, or until the sauce starts to thicken slightly.

Place the figs onto a baking sheet, sprinkle with the remaining sugar, and broil until the sugar is melted.

Spoon the oatmeal into individual bowls and top with a little milk, then divide the figs and the caramel sauce among the bowls. Top each serving with a large dollop of thick cream.

SERVES 4

mixed berry couscous

1 cup couscous
2 cups apple and cranberry juice
1 cinnamon stick
1¼ cups raspberries
1 cup blueberries
1¼ cups blackberries
1 cup strawberries, halved
zest of 1 lime
zest of 1 orange
¾ cup yogurt
2 tablespoons light corn or maple syrup
mint leaves, to garnish

Place the couscous in a bowl.

Place the apple and cranberry juice in a saucepan with the cinnamon stick. Bring to a boil, then remove from the heat and pour over the couscous. Cover with plastic wrap and allow to stand for 5 minutes, or until all the liquid has been absorbed. Remove and discard the cinnamon stick.

Separate the grains of the couscous with a fork, add the raspberries, blueberries, blackberries, strawberries, lime zest, and orange zest, and fold through gently. Spoon the mixture into four bowls and serve with a generous dollop of yogurt and a drizzle of light corn or maple syrup. Garnish with mint leaves.

SERVES 4

ginger and ricotta pancakes with fresh honeycomb

1 cup whole-wheat all-purpose flour
2 teaspoons baking powder
2 teaspoons ground ginger
2 tablespoons superfine sugar
1 cup flaked coconut, toasted
4 eggs, separated
1 lb ricotta cheese
1¼ cups milk
melted butter or oil, for brushing
4 bananas, sliced
7 oz fresh honeycomb, broken into large pieces

Sift the flour, baking powder, ginger, and sugar into a bowl. Stir in the coconut and make a well in the center of the mixture. Add the combined egg yolks, three-quarters of the ricotta, and all of the milk. Mix until smooth.

Beat the egg whites until soft peaks form, then gently fold into the pancake mixture.

Heat a skillet and brush lightly with a little melted butter or oil. Pour 3 tablespoons of the batter into the skillet and swirl gently to create an even pancake. Cook over low heat until bubbles form on the surface. Flip and cook the other side for 1 minute, or until golden. Continue until all the batter is used up.

Stack three pancakes onto each plate and top with a generous dollop of ricotta, 1 sliced banana, and a large piece of fresh honeycomb.

SERVES 4

chocolate-hazelnut puff pastry rolls

1/4 cup chocolate-hazelnut spread

2/3 cup confectioners' sugar, plus extra
   for rolling and dusting

2 sheets puff pastry, thawed

1 egg, lightly beaten

Preheat the oven to 400°F. Combine the chocolate-hazelnut spread and confectioners' sugar, and roll into an 8-inch-long roll. Wrap the roll in plastic wrap and twist the ends to enclose. Refrigerate for 30 minutes. When firm, cut the roll into eight even pieces. Roll each of the pieces in confectioners' sugar.

Cut each sheet of puff pastry into four squares. Place a piece of the chocolate-hazelnut roll onto each square of pastry, and roll up to enclose. Pinch the ends and brush lightly with egg. Bake for 15 minutes, or until the pastry is golden. Dust with confectioners' sugar.

SERVES 4

pecan phyllo sheets with fried apples

8 sheets phyllo pastry

1/4 cup melted butter

11/4 cups chopped pecans

1/4 cup soft brown sugar

1/4 cup plus 1 tablespoon unmelted butter

1/2 teaspoon freshly grated nutmeg, plus extra, for dusting

1 teaspoon ground cinnamon

1/4 teaspoon ground cloves

4 small Granny Smith apples, sliced into 1/2-inch-thick slices
horizontally (do not peel or core)

3/4 cup Neufchatel

Preheat the oven to 400°F. Brush one sheet of phyllo pastry with some of the melted butter. Top with another sheet, sprinkle with one-third of the pecans and sugar, top with another layer of phyllo, brush with more melted butter, and repeat the layering and sprinkling until you have used all the pastry, pecans, and sugar. Use scissors to cut the pastry in half, then cut each half into eight triangles. Place the triangles on two baking sheets and bake for 10 minutes, or until crisp and golden.

Heat the unmelted butter in a large skillet, add the spices and apples, and cook over medium heat for 5 minutes, turning the apples once, until they are soft and golden. Serve accompanied with the phyllo triangles and a spoonful of Neufchatel. Dust with nutmeg.

SERVES 4–6

star anise, lime, and vanilla tropical fruit salad

2¼ lb watermelon, cut into large pieces
1 small pineapple, chopped
2 mangoes, sliced
1 guava, sliced
1 small red papaya, cut into large pieces
12 lychees, peeled
3 kiwifruit, sliced
3 tablespoons lime juice
¾ cup grated jaggery or soft brown sugar
6 star anise
1 vanilla bean, split in half
1 pandanus leaf, knotted
zest of 1 lime

Place the watermelon, pineapple, mangoes, guava, papaya, lychees, and kiwifruit in a bowl and gently combine.

Place the lime juice, jaggery, star anise, vanilla bean, pandanus leaf, lime zest, and 1 cup of water in a saucepan and stir over low heat until the sugar dissolves. Bring to a boil, reduce the heat, and simmer for 10 minutes, or until the syrup is reduced by half. Allow to cool slightly.

Pour the syrup over the fruit and refrigerate until cold.

SERVES 6

pancakes with rose-water strawberries and butter

1½ cups self-rising flour
2 tablespoons plus 1 cup superfine sugar
pinch salt
2 eggs, lightly beaten
1 cup milk
¼ cup melted butter, plus extra for brushing
1 tablespoon ground cinnamon
2⅔ cups strawberries, halved
2 teaspoons rose water
1 teaspoon natural vanilla extract
3 tablespoons maple syrup
¼ cup plus 2 tablespoons unmelted butter, softened and whipped

Sift the flour, 2 tablespoons sugar, and pinch of salt into a bowl and make a well in the center. Mix together the eggs, milk, and ¼ cup melted butter in a pitcher, and pour into the well. Whisk to form a smooth batter. Cover and allow to stand for 20 minutes.

Heat a nonstick skillet and brush with the extra melted butter. Add 3 tablespoons of batter into the skillet and swirl gently. Cook over low heat for 1 minute, or until bubbles burst on the surface. Turn the pancake over and cook the other side. Transfer to a plate and keep warm while cooking the remaining batter.

Combine the 1 cup sugar and the cinnamon, and toss each pancake in the mixture. Combine the strawberries, rose water, vanilla, and maple syrup. Serve stacks of the pancakes topped with whipped butter and the strawberry mixture.

SERVES 4

high-top cappuccino and white-chocolate muffins

¼ cup instant espresso coffee powder

2½ cups self-rising flour

½ cup superfine sugar

2 eggs, lightly beaten

1½ cups buttermilk

1 teaspoon natural vanilla extract

⅔ cup melted butter

¾ cup chopped white chocolate

2 tablespoons unmelted butter

3 tablespoons soft brown sugar

Preheat the oven to 400°F. Cut eight lengths of baking paper and roll into 3-inch-high cylinders to fit into eight ½-cup ramekins. When in place in the ramekins, secure the cylinders with string, then place all the ramekins onto a baking sheet.

Dissolve the coffee in 1 tablespoon of boiling water and allow to cool. Sift the flour and superfine sugar into a bowl. Combine the eggs, buttermilk, vanilla, melted butter, white chocolate, and the coffee mixture, and roughly mix with the dry ingredients. Spoon the mixture into each cylinder. Heat the unmelted butter and brown sugar, and stir until the sugar dissolves. Spoon this mixture onto each muffin, and gently swirl into the muffin using a skewer. Bake for 25–30 minutes, or until risen and cooked through when tested with a skewer.

MAKES 8 MUFFINS

sweet

raspberry marshmallow muffins

1 cup all-purpose flour
1½ cups confectioners' sugar
1 cup ground hazelnuts
½ cup dried coconut
5 egg whites
¾ cup butter, melted and cooled
¾ cup raspberries
1 cup small pink marshmallows, chopped, plus 10 extra, whole

Preheat the oven to 400°F. Lightly grease a small 10-hole muffin pan.

Sift the flour and confectioners' sugar into a bowl. Stir in the ground hazelnuts and coconut.

Whisk the egg whites in a clean, dry bowl until foamy. Fold into the dry ingredients with the melted butter.

Set aside 20 of the raspberries, then carefully fold the rest into the mixture with the chopped marshmallows. Spoon into the pans. Press a whole marshmallow and two raspberries into the top of each muffin.

Bake for 20 minutes, or until golden and starting to come away from the sides of the pans. Leave to cool for 5 minutes in the pans before turning out onto a wire rack to cool completely.

MAKES 10 MUFFINS

rhubarb with vanilla and cardamom rice

4 cups milk
1 cup sugar
1 vanilla bean, split in half and seeds scraped out
4 cardamom pods, bruised
1 cup arborio rice
3/4 cup mascarpone cheese (optional)
3²/₃ cups rhubarb, cut into short lengths
1/2 cup soft brown sugar
1 cinnamon stick

Put the milk, sugar, vanilla bean, and cardamom in a saucepan and heat until just about to boil. Add the rice and cook, stirring, for 20–30 minutes, or until tender.

Add the mascarpone, if using, and beat until thick and creamy. Remove the vanilla bean and cardamom.

Put the rhubarb, brown sugar, cinnamon stick, and 3 tablespoons of water in a saucepan, cover with a tight-fitting lid, and cook over medium heat for 5 minutes. Stir and check to see how soft the rhubarb is. It should break into strands. If it doesn't, cook for a few more minutes, taking care not to overcook or it will become mushy. Serve with the creamed rice.

SERVES 4

banana, sunflower, and pistachio bread

¼ cup plus 2 tablespoons butter, softened
¾ cup brown sugar
2 eggs, lightly beaten
2½ cups ripe mashed bananas
¾ cup shelled pistachio nuts, roughly chopped
½ cup sunflower seeds
2 cups self-rising flour
1 teaspoon baking soda
½ teaspoon mixed (pumpkin pie) spice
butter and honey, to serve

Preheat the oven to 350°F. Grease and line the base of a 9-inch loaf pan.

Beat the butter and sugar until light and creamy. Add the eggs gradually, beating well after each addition. Stir in the bananas, nuts, and seeds.

Sift together the flour, baking soda, and mixed spice, then fold into the banana mixture.

Spoon into the pan and bake for 1 hour, or until a skewer comes out clean when inserted into the center. Leave to cool in the pan for 15 minutes before turning out onto a wire rack to cool completely. Serve buttered and drizzled with runny honey.

SERVES 6–8

passion fruit sugar muffins

2 1/2 cups self-rising flour
1 1/2 cups superfine sugar
1 1/2 cups buttermilk
2 eggs
1 teaspoon natural vanilla extract
1 cup butter, melted and cooled
1/4 cup passion fruit pulp
1–2 tablespoons lemon juice

Preheat the oven to 375°F. Lightly grease a twelve-hole muffin pan. Sift the flour into a bowl and stir in 1/2 cup of the sugar. Make a well in the center.

Whisk together the buttermilk, eggs, vanilla, and 2/3 cup of the melted butter, and pour into the well. Stir until only just combined (the mixture should still be lumpy).

Half-fill each muffin hole with mixture, then add 1 teaspoon of passion fruit pulp to each muffin and top off with the remaining mixture. Bake for 30 minutes, or until risen and springy to the touch.

Mix the lemon juice and remaining butter in a bowl, and spread the remaining sugar on a plate. Brush the warm muffins with lemon butter and roll in the sugar. Repeat and serve warm.

MAKES 12 MUFFINS

sweet

brioche eggy bread with figs and raspberry cream

4 small brioche rolls
3 eggs, lightly beaten
1 cup milk
1 teaspoon almond extract
1/4 cup butter
6 figs, quartered
2 tablespoons soft brown sugar

RASPBERRY CREAM
1²/₃ cups raspberries
3/4 cup sour cream
3 tablespoons soft brown sugar

Cut the brioche rolls lengthwise into thick slices. Whisk together the eggs, milk, and almond extract.

Heat half the butter in a large skillet. Dip a slice of brioche in the egg mixture, letting any extra drain off, then lay in the skillet. Fry over medium heat until golden brown on both sides. Keep warm while you cook the rest, adding more butter to the skillet as you need it.

Arrange the figs, cut side up, on a baking sheet, sprinkle lightly with the sugar, and broil until the sugar has caramelized and the figs have softened.

To make the raspberry cream, lightly crush the raspberries with a fork. Stir through the sour cream with the brown sugar. Serve with the brioche and figs.

SERVES 4

poached stone fruit

1 cup superfine sugar
1 cinnamon stick
3 star anise
6 cloves
1⅛ lb apricots
2¼ lb freestone peaches
1⅛ lb nectarines

Put the sugar, cinnamon stick, star anise, and cloves in a saucepan with 4 cups of water, and stir over low heat until the sugar has dissolved.

Bring to a boil, add the fruit, and simmer for 10 minutes, or until soft. Remove the fruit, peel, and halve.

Simmer the liquid for 10 minutes, or until thickened slightly.

Place the fruit in a bowl, pour the syrup over the top, and leave to cool. Store in a vacuum-sealed glass jar in the fridge for up to three weeks.

Serve with thick yogurt or on top of breakfast cereal.

SERVES 6–8

creamed rice with minted citrus compote

¾ cup basmati rice
2 cups milk
4 cardamom pods, bruised
½ cinnamon stick
1 clove
3 tablespoons honey
1 teaspoon natural vanilla extract

MINTED CITRUS COMPOTE
2 pink grapefruit, segmented
2 oranges, segmented
3 tablespoons orange juice
1 teaspoon grated lime zest
3 tablespoons honey
8 mint leaves, finely chopped

Cook the rice in a large saucepan with 1 cup of boiling water for 12 minutes, stirring occasionally. Drain and cool.

Place the rice, milk, cardamom pods, cinnamon stick, and clove in a saucepan, and bring to a boil. Reduce the heat to low and simmer for 15 minutes, stirring occasionally, until the milk is absorbed and the rice is creamy. Remove the spices, then stir in the honey and vanilla.

To make the compote, combine the pink grapefruit, oranges, orange juice, lime zest, honey, and mint, and mix until the honey has dissolved. Serve with the rice.

SERVES 4

blueberry pancakes

1 cup buttermilk
1 egg, lightly beaten
1 tablespoon butter, melted
1 teaspoon natural vanilla extract
¾ cup all-purpose flour
1 teaspoon baking powder
½ teaspoon sea salt
2 ripe bananas, mashed
⅔ cup blueberries, plus extra, to serve
1 teaspoon oil
maple syrup, to serve

Put the buttermilk, egg, butter, and vanilla extract in a bowl and whisk together. Sift in the flour, baking powder, and salt, then stir, making sure not to overblend; the batter should be lumpy. Add the fruit.

Heat the oil in a skillet over medium heat. Add 2 tablespoons of batter to the skillet for each pancake. Cook for 3 minutes, or until the pancakes are golden brown on the bottom. Turn over and cook for an additional minute. Repeat with the rest of the batter, keeping the cooked pancakes warm. Serve immediately, with extra blueberries and maple syrup.

MAKES ABOUT 12 PANCAKES

sweet

broiled nectarines with cinnamon toast

3 tablespoons low-fat margarine
1 teaspoon ground cinnamon
4 thick slices brioche
6 ripe nectarines, halved and stones removed
confectioners' sugar, to serve
2 tablespoons warmed blossom honey

Place the margarine and cinnamon in a bowl and mix until well combined. Broil the brioche on one side until golden. Spread the other side with half the cinnamon spread, then broil until golden. Keep warm in the oven.

Brush the nectarines with the remaining spread and cook under a broiler or on a ridged grill plate until the spread is bubbling and the fruit is tinged at the edges.

To serve, place three nectarine halves on each toasted slice of brioche. Dust with the confectioners' sugar and drizzle with the warmed honey.

SERVES 4

NOTE: Canned plums or apricots may be used in place of nectarines.

raspberry breakfast crepes

2 cups all-purpose flour
1 teaspoon sugar
pinch salt
2 eggs, lightly beaten
2 cups milk
1 tablespoon butter, melted
3⅓ cups raspberries
confectioners' sugar, for dusting
maple syrup or honey, to serve

Sift the flour, sugar, and pinch of salt into a bowl and make a well in the center. In a bowl, mix the eggs and milk together with ⅓ cup plus 2 tablespoons of water. Slowly pour the mixture into the well, whisking all the time to incorporate the flour and ensure a smooth batter. Stir in the melted butter. Cover and refrigerate for 20 minutes.

Heat a crepe pan or a small nonstick skillet over medium heat and lightly grease. Pour in enough batter to coat the base of the skillet in a thin, even layer. Tip out any excess. Cook for 1 minute, or until the crepe starts to come away from the side of the skillet. Turn over and cook on the other side for an additional minute, or until just golden. Repeat the process, stacking the crepes on a plate with waxed paper between them and covered with foil, until all the batter is used up.

To serve, put one crepe on a plate. Arrange some raspberries on a quarter of the crepe. Fold the crepe in half, then in half again, so that the raspberries are wrapped in a triangular pocket. Repeat with the remaining crepes and raspberries. Dust with confectioners' sugar and drizzle with maple syrup or honey.

MAKES 8 LARGE CREPES

sweet

spiced fruit salad

½ cup superfine sugar
4 slices ginger
1 bird's-eye chili, cut in half
juice and zest of 2 limes
mixed fruit—such as watermelon, cantaloupe, mango, banana,
    cherries, lychees, and kiwifruit—enough for four portions

Put the sugar in a saucepan with ½ cup of water, the ginger, and the chili. Heat until the sugar melts, then leave to cool before adding the lime juice and zest. Remove the ginger and chili.

Put your selection of fruit into a bowl and pour over the syrup. Leave to marinate in the refrigerator for 30 minutes before serving.

SERVES 4

apple and berry crumble muffins

1¼ cups self-rising flour
1 cup whole-wheat self-rising flour
¼ teaspoon ground cinnamon
pinch ground cloves
½ cup firmly packed soft brown sugar
¾ cup milk
2 eggs
½ cup unsalted butter, melted and cooled
2 Granny Smith apples, peeled and grated
1 cup blueberries

CRUMBLE
⅓ cup all-purpose flour
¼ cup raw sugar
⅓ cup rolled oats
4 tablespoons unsalted butter, chopped

Preheat the oven to 375°F. Line a twelve-hole muffin pan with muffin papers. Sift the flours, cinnamon, and cloves into a large bowl and stir in the brown sugar. Make a well in the center of the mixture.

Put the milk, eggs, and butter in a bowl, whisk, and pour into the well. Fold until just combined, then fold in the fruit. Divide among the muffin holes.

To make the crumble, put the flour, sugar, and oats in a bowl. Rub the butter in with your fingertips until most of the lumps are gone. Sprinkle 2 teaspoons of the crumble over each muffin. Bake for 25 minutes, or until golden. Cool for 5 minutes, then transfer to a wire rack.

MAKES 12 MUFFINS

sweet

apricot and raisin bran loaf

¾ cup dried apricots, chopped
1 cup raisins
1 cup bran flakes
½ cup soft brown sugar
1½ cups warm milk
1 cup self-rising flour, sifted
½ cup whole-wheat self-rising flour, sifted
1 teaspoon mixed (pumpkin pie) spice

Preheat the oven to 350°F. Lightly grease a deep 7¼ inch x 4¼ inch loaf pan and line the base and sides with baking paper.

Soak the apricots, raisins, bran flakes, and brown sugar in the milk in a large bowl for 30 minutes, or until the milk is almost completely absorbed. Stir in the flours and mixed spice to form a stiff, moist batter. Spoon the mixture into the pan and smooth the surface.

Bake for 50 minutes, or until a skewer comes out clean when inserted into the center of the loaf—cover with foil during cooking if it browns too much. Leave in the pan for 10 minutes, then turn out onto a wire rack to cool. Cut into thick slices. If desired, serve with butter and dust with confectioners' sugar.

SERVES 6–8

NOTE: Use any dried fruit combination. This loaf is delicious toasted.

sticky gingerbread muffins

2 cups self-rising flour, sifted
¾ cup all-purpose flour, sifted
½ teaspoon baking soda
1 tablespoon ground ginger
1 teaspoon ground cinnamon
1 teaspoon mixed (pumpkin pie) spice
1 cup firmly packed soft brown sugar
¼ cup chopped crystallized ginger
⅔ cup light corn or maple syrup
¼ cup plus 2 tablespoons unsalted butter, chopped
1 cup buttermilk
1 egg, lightly beaten

Preheat the oven to 400°F. Lightly grease a twelve-hole muffin pan.
Put the flours, baking soda, ginger, cinnamon, and mixed spice in a bowl.
Stir in the brown sugar and crystallized ginger.

Melt the light corn or maple syrup and butter in a saucepan. Cool.
Combine the syrup mixture, buttermilk, and egg, and pour into the well.
Fold until just combined.

Divide the mixture among the muffin holes. Bake for 20–25 minutes, or
until the muffins come away from the side of the hole. Cool for 5 minutes
in the hole, then transfer to a wire rack to cool completely.

MAKES 12 MUFFINS

chewy fruit and seed slice

¾ cup plus 2 tablespoons unsalted butter

½ cup light corn or maple syrup

½ cup crunchy peanut butter

2 teaspoons natural vanilla extract

¼ cup all-purpose flour

⅓ cup ground almonds

½ teaspoon mixed (pumpkin pie) spice

3 cups quick-cooking oats

2 teaspoons finely grated orange zest

1 cup soft brown sugar

½ cup dried coconut

⅓ cup sesame seeds, toasted

½ cup pepitas or shelled sunflower seeds

½ cup raisins, chopped

¼ cup mixed candied orange and lemon peel

Preheat the oven to 325°F. Lightly grease a 8 inch x 12 inch shallow pan and line with baking paper, leaving it hanging over the two long sides.

Place the butter and light corn or maple syrup in a small saucepan over low heat, stirring occasionally until melted. Remove from the heat and stir in the peanut butter and vanilla until combined.

In a separate bowl, mix together the remaining ingredients, stirring well. Make a well in the center and add the butter and syrup mixture. Mix with a large metal spoon until combined. Press evenly into the pan and bake for 25 minutes, or until golden and firm. Cool in the pan, then cut into squares.

MAKES 18 PIECES

blueberry muffins

3 cups all-purpose flour
1 tablespoon baking powder
¾ cup firmly packed soft brown sugar
½ cup unsalted butter, melted
2 eggs, lightly beaten
1 cup milk
1¼ cups fresh or thawed frozen blueberries

Preheat the oven to 415°F. Lightly grease a twelve-hole muffin pan. Sift the flour and baking powder into a large bowl. Stir in the sugar and make a well in the center.

Add the combined melted butter, eggs, and milk all at once, and fold until just combined. Do not overmix—the batter should look quite lumpy.

Fold in the blueberries. Spoon the batter into the prepared pan. Bake for 20 minutes, or until golden brown. Cool on a wire rack.

MAKES 12 MUFFINS

banana and honey loaf

½ cup unsalted butter, softened
¾ cup soft brown sugar
2 eggs, lightly beaten
2 tablespoons honey
1 large ripe banana, cut into chunks
1½ cups whole-wheat self-rising flour
2 teaspoons ground cinnamon

Preheat the oven to 350°F. Lightly grease an 8½ inch x 4½ inch loaf pan. Combine the butter and sugar in a food processor for 1 minute, or until lighter in color. Add the egg and process until combined.

Put 1 tablespoon of the honey in a saucepan over low heat and warm for 1 minute, or until runny. Add to the food processor with the banana and blend until smooth. Add the flour and cinnamon, and process until well combined.

Spoon evenly into the pan and bake for 35–40 minutes, or until a skewer comes out clean when inserted into the center of the loaf. Leave in the pan for 5 minutes before turning out onto a wire rack. Warm the remaining honey in a saucepan over low heat for 1 minute, or until runny. Brush the warm loaf with the warm honey. Serve warm or cool.

SERVES 8

VARIATION: Fold ½ cup chopped walnuts or pecans through the mixture before spooning the mixture into the loaf pan.

red fruit salad with berries

SYRUP
¼ cup superfine sugar
½ cup dry red wine
1 star anise
1 teaspoon finely chopped lemon zest

1⅔ cups strawberries, hulled and halved
1 cup blueberries
1¼ cups raspberries, mulberries, or other red berries
1¼ cups cherries
5 small red plums, pitted and quartered
yogurt, to serve

To make the syrup, place the sugar, wine, star anise, lemon zest, and ½ cup of water in a small saucepan. Bring to a boil over medium heat, stirring to dissolve the sugar. Boil the syrup for 3 minutes, then set aside to cool for 30 minutes. When cool, strain the syrup.

Mix the fruit together in a large bowl and pour on the red wine syrup. Mix well to coat the fruit in the syrup and refrigerate for 1½ hours. Serve the fruit dressed with a little syrup and the yogurt.

SERVES 6

broiled figs with ricotta

2 tablespoons honey
1 cinnamon stick
3 tablespoons flaked almonds
4 large (or 8 small) figs
1/2 cup ricotta cheese
1/2 teaspoon natural vanilla extract
2 tablespoons confectioners' sugar, sifted
pinch of ground cinnamon
1/2 teaspoon finely grated orange zest

Place the honey and cinnamon stick in a small saucepan with 4 tablespoons of water. Bring to a boil, then reduce the heat and simmer gently for 6 minutes, or until thickened and reduced by half. Discard the cinnamon stick and stir in the almonds.

Preheat the broiler to hot and grease a shallow ovenproof dish large enough to fit all the figs side by side. Slice the figs into quarters from the top to within 1/2 inch of the bottom, keeping them attached at the base. Arrange in the prepared dish.

Combine the ricotta, vanilla, confectioners' sugar, ground cinnamon, and orange zest in a small bowl. Divide the filling among the figs, spooning it into their cavities. Spoon the syrup over the top. Place under the broiler and cook until the juices start to come out from the figs and the almonds are lightly toasted. Cool for 2–3 minutes. Spoon the juices and any fallen almonds from the bottom of the dish over the figs and serve.

SERVES 4

index

A
apple and berry crumble
    muffins 141
apricot
  and bran breakfast shake
    10, 93
  and raisin bran loaf 142
arugula
  arugula, mushroom, and
    blue cheese omelet 53
  fried halloumi, tomato,
    and arugula
    sandwiches 54
asparagus
  potato flowers with
    salmon, quail eggs,
    and 42
  steamed, with crispy
    pancetta and hard-
    boiled quail eggs 10

B
bagels with smoked salmon
    and caper salsa 30
banana
  banana, sunflower, and
    pistachio bread 122
  creamy rich banana and
    macadamia smoothie
    94
  and honey loaf 150
  with light corn syrup
    and macadamia nuts 8
  and mango with vanilla
    soy milk and honey-
    drizzled yogurt 12
bell pepper and sweet
    potato rosti with pork
    sausages 21
berry couscous, mixed 105

blt, mediterranean 14
blueberry
  muffins 149
  pancakes 133
bran loaf, apricot and
    raisin 142
bread, banana, sunflower,
    and pistachio 122
breakfast shake, apricot
    and bran 10, 93
brioche eggy bread with
    figs and raspberry
    cream 126
broiled portobello
    mushrooms with garlic
    and chili 66
broiled figs with ricotta
    154
broiled nectarines with
    cinnamon toast 134
bruschetta with salmon
    tartare and roe 50

C
caffe latte
  cardamom, with
    frangelico 13
  decadent, infused with a
    vanilla bean 12
cappuccino and white-
    chocolate muffins,
    high-top 117
caramelized leek, goat
    cheese, and spinach
    pie 38
champagne with
    strawberries and
    blackberries 13
cheese and onion waffles
    with herbed ricotta

and roasted tomato 61
cheese soufflés, twice-
    baked 41
chewy fruit and seed slice
    146
chocolate-hazelnut puff
    pastry rolls 109
cinnamon oatmeal with
    caramel figs and cream
    102
cinnamon toast, broiled
    nectarines with 134
citrus compote, minted,
    with creamed rice 130
classic omelet 82
corn
  fritters with crispy
    prosciutto 22
  squiggly corn crab cakes
    46
couscous, mixed berry 105
crab cakes, squiggly corn 46
creamed rice with minted
    citrus compote 130
crepes, raspberry breakfast
    137
crispy lavash tiles with
    butter mushrooms 34
crispy prosciutto
  corn fritters with 22
  french toast with 62
croissants, scrambled eggs
    and salmon on 57
croque madame 73

D
dates, figs, and pine nuts
    on honey-drizzled
    yogurt 11
dried fruit slices 11

E

eggs
  benedict 26
  fried, and red onion
    wrap 78
  fried, and tomatoes on
    scallion potato cakes
    65
  scrambled, and salmon
    on brioche 57
  scrambled, with cheese
    and herb corn bread
    29
  smoked ham, egg, and
    jarlsberg cheese
    sandwiches 25

F

figs
  brioche eggy bread with
    figs and raspberry
    cream 126
  broiled, with ricotta
    154
  cinnamon oatmeal with
    caramel figs and cream
    102
  and dates with honey-
    drizzled yogurt and
    pine nuts 11
finger bananas, halved,
    with light corn syrup
    and macadamia nuts
    8
french toast with crispy
    prosciutto 62
fried eggs
  and red onion wrap 78
  tomatoes and, on
    scallion potato cakes
    65
fried green tomatoes with
    halloumi 18
fried halloumi, tomato,
    and arugula
    sandwiches 54

frittatas
  mini sweet potato and
    leek 86
  salmon, dill, and
    camembert 17
fritters, corn, with crispy
    prosciutto 22
fruit, winter, in orange
    ginger syrup 157
fruit platter 10
fruit salad
  red, with berries 153
  spiced 138
  star anise, lime, and
    vanilla tropical 113

G

ginger ale and pineapple
    juice punch with
    ginger, strawberries,
    and mint leaves 12
ginger and ricotta
    pancakes with
    honeycomb 106
gingerbread muffins, sticky
    145
ginger tea with lemongrass
    swizzle sticks 13
goat cheese
  herbed garlic
    mushrooms with goat
    cheese bruschetta 85
  spinach pie, caramelized
    leek and 38
granola, healthy nut and
    seed 101
gravlax with parmesan
    sheets 49

H

halloumi
  fried green tomatoes
    with 18
  fried halloumi, tomato,
    and arugula
    sandwiches 54

ham, egg, and jarlsberg
    cheese sandwiches 25
healthy nut and seed
    granola 101
herbed garlic mushrooms
    with goat cheese
    bruschetta 85
high-top cappuccino and
    white-chocolate
    muffins 117
honey-drizzled yogurt
  banana and mango
    blended with vanilla
    soy and 12
  figs, dates, and pine nuts
    with 11
huevos rancheros 74

I

iced chocolate 8
individual herbed lemon
    ricotta 37

K

kedgeree 90

L

lavash tiles, crispy, with
    butter mushrooms
    34
leeks
  caramelized leek, goat
    cheese, and spinach
    pie 38
  mini sweet potato and
    leek frittatas 86
loaf
  apricot and raisin
    bran 142
  banana and honey 150

M

mango and banana with
    vanilla soy milk and
    honey-drizzled yogurt
    12

maple yogurt balls with
 sugary balsamic pears
 98
mediterranean blt 14
mini savory breakfast pies
 58
mini sweet potato and leek
 frittatas 86
minted citrus compote
 with creamed rice 130
mixed berry couscous 105
muffins
 apple and berry crumble
  141
 blueberry 149
 high-top cappuccino
  and white-chocolate
  117
 passion fruit sugar 125
 raspberry marshmallow
  118
 sticky gingerbread 145
mushrooms
 arugula, mushroom, and
  blue cheese omelet 53
 broiled portobello, with
  garlic and chili 66
 butter, crispy lavash tiles
  with 34
 herbed garlic, with goat
  cheese bruschetta 85
 marinated feta with 45
 omelet with chorizo 70

O
oatmeal, cinnamon, with
 caramel figs and cream
 102
omelets
 arugula, mushroom, and
  blue cheese 53
 classic 82
 mushroom, with chorizo
  70
 spanish, with smoked
  salmon 77

P
pancakes
 blueberry 133
 ginger and ricotta, with
  fresh honeycomb 106
 with rose-water
  strawberries and butter
  114
pandoro with poached
 peaches and
 mascarpone 97
panettone, toasted, with
 sweet sage, apple, and
 cinnamon toddies 8
papaya, red, drizzled with
 tangy lime juice 10
passion fruit sugar muffins
 125
peaches, poached, pandoro
 with mascarpone and
 97
pears, maple yogurt balls
 with 98
pecan phyllo sheets with
 fried apples 110
pies
 mini savory breakfast 58
 spinach, caramelized leek,
  and goat cheese 38
pineapple and star fruit
 slices with maple syrup
 and shaved toasted
 coconut 11
pineapple juice and ginger
 ale punch with ginger,
 strawberries, and mint
 leaves 12
piperade 69
poached peaches, pandoro
 with mascarpone and
 97
poached stone fruits 129
pomegranates, red,
 drizzled with rose
 water and apple juice
 11

potato
 cakes, scallion, fried eggs,
  and tomatoes on 65
 flowers with salmon,
  asparagus, and quail
  eggs 42
 patties, salmon and dill,
  with lime mayonnaise
  81
 tortilla 89
prosciutto, crispy
 corn fritters with 22
 french toast with 62
puff pastry rolls,
 chocolate-hazelnut 109

Q
quail eggs
 hard-boiled, with
  steamed asparagus and
  crispy pancetta 10
 potato flowers with
  salmon, asparagus, and
  42

R
raspberry
 breakfast crepes 137
 brioche eggy bread with
  figs and raspberry
  cream 126
 marshmallow muffins 118
red fruit salad with berries
 153
rhubarb with vanilla and
 cardamom rice 121
rice
 creamed, with minted
  citrus compote 130
 vanilla and cardamom,
  with rhubarb 121
ricotta, individual herbed
 lemon 37
rosti, sweet potato and bell
 pepper, with pork
 sausages 21